ABOVE CHICAGO

by ROBERT CAMERON

A new collection of historical and original
aerial photographs of Chicago

with text by
Tim Samuelson and Cheryl Kent

CAMERON and COMPANY, San Francisco, California

Such a book as this does not reach publication without more than the usual cooperation
from many people. So, for their encouragement and expertise, I thank the following:

Victor Abnee, Hatsuro Aizawa, Susan Benjamin, Davis Butler, Robert Burger, Anthony Cameron, Phoebe Cameron,
Todd Cameron, Madelaine Cassidy, Dan Chichester, James Dau, Robert Ekstrand, Marshall Field, John Goy, Tina Hodge,
Tim Hoover, Blair Kamin, David King, Robert Maldonado, Robert Meiborg, Patricia O'Grady, Harry Price,
Maurice Ross Jr., Dorothy Ross and Michael R. V. Whitman.

Special mention goes to helicopter pilot Bob Kenney of Omniflight who knows his aircraft
and knows Chicago, above which he has flown for thousands of hours.

The research and writing of the captions were the work of Tim Samuelson and Cheryl Kent.
I was lucky to find such knowledgeable and talented people.

For assistance in researching the historical aerial photography, acknowledgement is made to:
The Art Institute of Chicago Archives for pages 8, 16, 20, 32, 52,
The David R. Phillips Collection for pages 10, 12, 78, 102, 114, 146,
Chicago Aerial Survey Company for pages 24, 26, 52, 62, 70, 92, 110,
and Weigel Aerial Survey, Page 90.

The National Aeronautics and Space Administration, Ames Research Center.

CAMERON and COMPANY

680 8TH STREET, SUITE 205 SAN FRANCISCO CA 94103   800-779-5582   www.abovebooks.com

Library of Congress Catalog Number: 92-93090
Above Chicago ISBN 0-918684-27-7
© 1992 by Robert W. Cameron and Company, Inc. All rights reserved.

First Printing, 1992
Second Printing, 1992
Third Printing, 1996
Fourth Printing, 1997
Fifth Printing, 2000
Sixth Printing, 2001
Seventh Printing, 2004

Book design by
JANE OLAUG KRISTIANSEN

Color processing by The New Lab, San Francisco, Ross-Ehlert Lab, Chicago
Camera Work by Copy Service, San Francisco
Photo Retouching by Alicemarie Mutrux and Jerome Vloeberghs, San Francisco
Printed in Hong Kong

TABLE OF CONTENTS

(Caption for page 7) There's no mistaking it. This is Chicago. Seen across the low-rise, hardworking West Side, the legendary skyscrapers of downtown rise up from the flat midwestern plain. Chicago has always been famous for building tall. It has erected the world's tallest building twice. The current champion is Sears Tower. Some say Chicago has built big in order to invent a landscape where there was none. But maybe they weren't taking into account the extreme and changing beauty of Lake Michigan which composes the city's backdrop.

I was born and raised in the Midwest. Where I grew up, everyone thought of Chicago as our big town. It meant excitement to me. It still does.

Ah, those trips to Chicago! My parents took me to the city when I was a boy. By the 1930s, when I was making my own decisions, I went back – for the music and the friends I had made there. Chicago was a world center for jazz then, which had travelled up the river from New Orleans and I was just the right age to be mesmerized by it. Earl Hines was at the Grand Terrace. Roy Eldridge was at the Three Deuces. Benny Goodman was at the Congress introducing swing to Chicago. And Louis Armstrong was everywhere. I was also at the right age to marry and get a job in the photography department of the *Des Moines Register.* Thus began my career in photography, which, happily, is not quite over.

Chicago's charms still hold me. It is, in many circles, considered to be the most architecturally distinguished city in the world – a fact that will be impressed upon anyone turning the pages of this book. But let me reminisce for a moment and allow the text to speak for itself.

I have been in love with photography ever since my father taught me how to ignite flash powder at the age of ten. When I started at the *Des Moines Register,* I was a darkroom rat. Eventually, I was elevated to news photographer. By that time, the flashbulb – filled with aluminum foil – had been invented. Sometimes it worked and sometimes it didn't. When it didn't, it exploded in the subject's face.

During World War II, I worked as a photographer for the War Department. I was 4-F, so I worked as a civilian, photographing army camps and installations in the United States. I did my first significant aerial work during the War. Those shots may not have been as good as the ones in this book, but I was hooked.

After the War, I thought of becoming a professional aerial photographer, but there were lots of us by then. Uncle Sam had produced thousands of aerial photographers who had experience like mine. By then I had a family to raise, so I built a business of my own in New York and made photography my hobby instead. It wasn't until the late 1960s, when helicopters had been perfected, that I came back to photography full-time when I moved my family to San Francisco. I started a new business – a publishing company. My first book was *Above San Francisco,* and it set a model for all books that followed. Since then I've done a dozen more, from Hawaii to Paris.

In making those books, I have tried every aerial device except hang gliders. I have flown and photographed from blimps (stable but clumsy), gliders (cramped), balloons (noisy and capricious), and fixed-wing planes. Helicopters are best and safest. With a good pilot, I can frame a shot while he hovers. Fixed high-wing planes are second best, but you have to grab shots and make another pass if you don't get what you want on the first try. I even photographed Yosemite through the windshield of a Falcon Jet at 45,000 feet. I lost some definition, but you can't take the door off up there.

Anyone who has ever flown knows that cities look completely different from the air. Not only is there a change in perspective, there is a change in relationships. It is always surprising to see, for example, that one's house has *this* geographical relationship to *that* shopping center, and not the one we have in our mind's eye when we're on the ground in our car. There is something else – less tangible. Airborne, man undergoes a subtle shift in values. What is important and significant on the ground seems strangely irrelevant a mile up, and what seemed like folly or even madness takes on some of the qualities of poetry when you're flying. My camera lens lets people experience their city in a new way.

When I started aerial photography, I used a Speed Graphic camera, which, under ideal circumstances, can be used at one-one-thousandth of a second. The Speed Graphic was a standard old news photographer's camera. It's still used to some extent. Then I used a 4x5 Linhof aerial camera, a format I still resort to in some situations. Ansel Adams tried to convert me to the Hasselblad, but I don't like square pictures – except his, of course. I generally use a 6x7 centimeter format; I have several of these cameras made by Pentax. And I use six lenses ranging from the fisheye to the four-hundred millimeter.

But the most important piece of equipment to my work is the Kenyon gyrostabilizer, which defeats vibration. To film or photograph from the air, most cinematographers use a mount which is part of the helicopter. The mount makes the equipment steady. My method is a little different. I always work with a hand-held camera and the gyrostabilizer attached to it. The gyrostabilizer is the shape of a large egg and weighs about ten pounds. It is sealed; inside, two gyros are whirling in a vacuum about two inches in diameter. One is whirling vertically, the other horizontally. They counterbalance each other. After about eight minutes on a six-volt battery, the gyros build up to 22,000 rpm. At this speed the gyrostabilizer becomes a thing in itself, unaffected by outside movement. It has its own mind, separate from the gravity of the earth and vibration. It holds the camera steady so

I can get the shots I want without worrying about the movement of the helicopter.

When I take a photograph, I am held in the helicopter by a harness. I sometimes must lean out of the aircraft. It is a sight that startles some people. When I was working on a book on Yosemite, I photographed three climbers halfway up the face of El Capitan. Now, you must understand, a good climber takes three days to get to the top of El Capitan. It is 3,000 feet high and presents a nearly sheer face. I was happy with the picture I took, and a few days later my pilot introduced me to the climbers when we happened to run into them back on the ground. One of them said to me, "Oh, were you the guy hanging out of a helicopter taking pictures of us? I wouldn't do that for all the tea in China."

I have had extraordinary moments in working on each book I have done. Not all of them have been triumphs. In Hawaii, I spent day after day flying over a volcano, watching it erupt and waiting for dark. Each night, the lava flow would stop as soon as night fell. I waited until my printers refused to hold the press any longer. Although I did get some good ones, I never got exactly the shot I wanted.

In Paris, I was told no one could fly within the Peripherique, Paris's belt parkway. What would my book be without central Paris? It took the intervention of Pierre Salinger with President François Mitterrand before I could fly within the Peripherique. My pilot didn't know where the buildings I wanted to photograph were. "How could I know," he asked, "I never have a chance to fly inside of Paris." There were many frustrating days in Paris, but finally, I made some of the best photographs I ever have, and, in my prints, I got the beautiful soft French light Monet and other Impressionists celebrated.

But Chicago has a light all its own!

I tried to do the impossible, covering the city in 153 pages. There's no way to do that, so I gave you a sampling, an evocative series of pictures of a world-class city. I think the beauty of this lakefront metropolis takes on a new meaning from the air. What becomes clear flying above it is that Chicago extends far beyond the political boundaries that technically define it. And the natural mother of the whole area is Lake Michigan.

We are living in a period of great transition. Man seems eager, and possibly able, to expand his view of himself and the dwelling places he has built, to include the earth and the universe. From above, the city landmarks take their place within the larger whole, of which man is an interesting, inspirational, often bewildered, but – let's face it – microscopic part.

– R.C.

THE LAKE FRONT

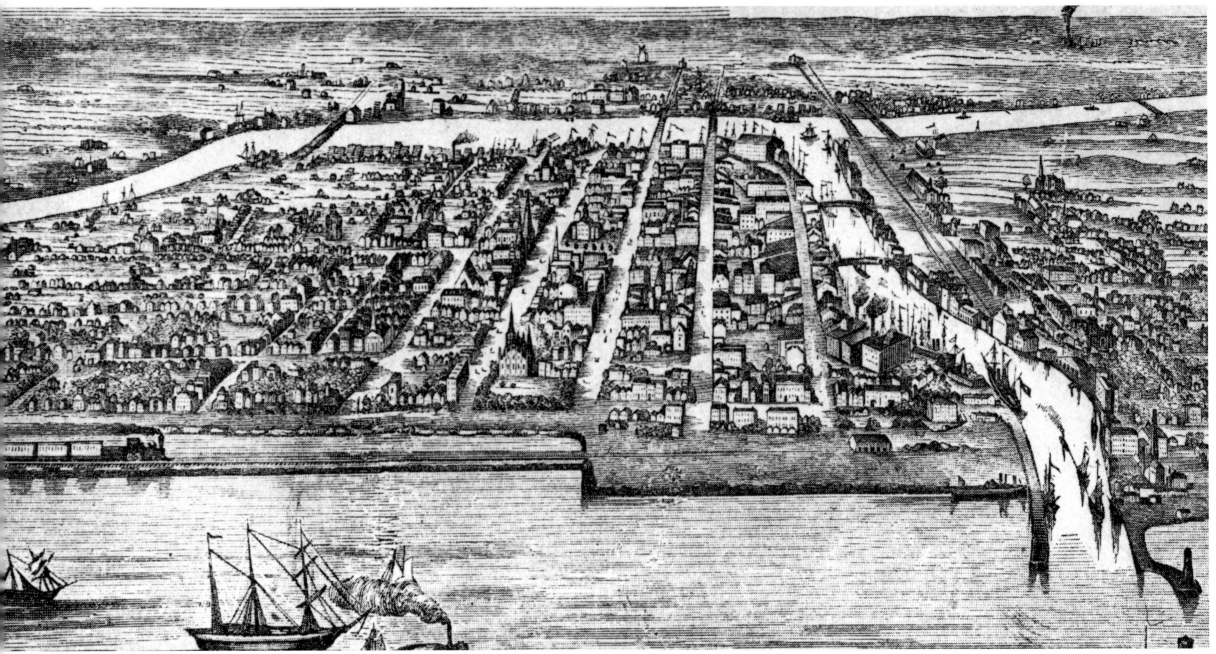

This is where Chicago began, at the juncture of Lake Michigan and the Chicago River. From a population of less than fifty in the early 1830s, Chicago had grown to more than thirty-thousand by 1853 when this was drawn. To the left of the Chicago River is the relatively small area which was and remains the heart of the city's central business district. The River's role as commercial artery is demonstrated by the factories and warehouses shown lining its banks. The Illinois Central Railroad originally entered the city on an open trestle built in the lake. It was left high and dry by landfill and subsequent fills moved it further and further inland.

(Opposite) The confluence of the Chicago River and Lake Michigan hardly resembles what it was a century and a half ago. Once a brackish stand of water, the mouth of the River has been shifted east by landfill and reshaped by massive public works projects. Even the direction of the River has been changed, the result of an astounding engineering feat completed in 1900. By closing the river mouth with locks and digging deep diversion channels in outlying areas, the Chicago River's sewage-filled flow was shifted away from the city's drinking water source, Lake Michigan, to a course that eventually empties into the Mississippi River.

In 1909, architect and planner Daniel Hudson Burnham presented his visionary Plan of Chicago to civic leaders. Among his recommendations was the construction of outlying recreational islands along the south lakefront. One was eventually built and is shown in this photograph, taken in 1929 when the Adler Planetarium was under construction. Within a short time the Planetarium was joined by the temporary buildings and grounds of the 1933-1934 world's fair.

(Opposite) The location of the Adler Planetarium was in keeping with the Burnham Plan; the decision to use the rest of the island for Miegs Field municipal airport was not. Burnham imagined the lakefront reserved for public, recreational and cultural uses. Miegs is used primarily by private business aircraft, introducing a commercial – to say nothing of noisy – element. Additions to the Planetarium have been placed underground so as not to violate the building's elegant domed profile.

In defiance of the Depression, Chicago celebrated its centennial by hosting the world's fair in 1933 and 1934. It was optimistically called the Century of Progress Exposition and – ominous predictions of failure notwithstanding – it was a success. In spite of the hard times, people from around the country came to see the futuristic fairgrounds located on the city's near-south-side lakefront. The buildings were demolished after the fair closed, but the infrastructure was later used to construct Miegs Field airport.

(Opposite) Lake Michigan landfill makes an appropriate foundation for the aquarium. Named for its founder, the John G. Shedd Aquarium opened in 1929. The 1991 addition of the wavelike Oceanarium at the rear gives Chicagoans views of dolphins, whales and other saltwater natives. The meandering green lawns of Burnham Park extend southward along the lakeshore following Daniel Burnham's recommendations for a recreational lakefront. It is doubtful, however, that the placement of the McCormick Place convention center, seen in the distance, would have been approved by the park's namesake.

Downtown workers lucky enough to secure a mooring in Monroe Harbor need only walk across Grant Park to take an after-hours sail on Lake Michigan.

(Opposite) Flying north toward the central business district, the tall buildings of downtown Chicago stand grouped in splendid isolation, a graphic demonstration of the city's compact development. For over a century, the combination of heavy river traffic, tightly held industrial districts and railroads confined the downtown to a relatively small area south and east of the Chicago River. The demand for scarce real estate and downtown's inability to expand laterally gave birth to the skyscraper in the late-nineteenth century. With river traffic now virtually nonexistent and the relocation of railroads and industrial areas, downtown Chicago has started to move outside its traditional boundaries.

This late-1920s view shows Grant Park in an early stage with newly laid formal gardens and promenades. Lake Shore Drive — defined here by a border of wispy trees — was originally intended for leisurely drives and has become, instead, a raceway for commuters.

(Opposite) Grant Park is Chicago's front yard. Through hard-won legislation it has been kept free of buildings for more than a mile between Randolph Street and Roosevelt Road. An exception was made for the original 1892 Art Institute. Expansion of the museum has been permitted but only after close scrutiny by the city and nearby property owners. The park's grassy expanses mask its infrastructure which includes underground parking garages and the recessed tracks of the Illinois Central Railroad. A sure sign of summer's beginning and end is Buckingham Fountain's start-up and shut-down.

The city's drinking water is pumped from circular cribs located two miles away from shore. The distinction of the loneliest job in Chicago could be held by the crew of three that arrives by motor launch to maintain the cribs in seven-hour shifts.

(Opposite) Two enormous public works projects erected a half century apart reach out to take advantage of Lake Michigan's manifold offerings. Navy Pier was completed in 1916 as a shipping and recreational facility. There, Chicagoans traded hot summer air for cool lake breezes. The center of the Pier originally held cargo sheds, but diminishing lake trade left them underused and they were demolished for a new development. To its right is the expansive 1972 Jardine Water Filtration Plant, the primary purification plant for the central city's water.

53980

Streeterville was named after the eccentric Captain George Wellington Streeter. In 1886 when Streeter's grounded boat was silted in at the shore near Superior Street, the Captain named the marshy patch the "District of Lake Michigan" and declared its independence. This he vigorously defended with his shotgun and wife Ma Streeter's boiling pails of water. After years of skirmishes and legal wrangling, the fight ended when the Captain died in 1921. The north end of Streeter's domain became Northwestern University's Chicago campus, shown in relative isolation in this 1929 view.

(Opposite) The original gothic buildings of Northwestern University's downtown campus have been obscured by new structures. One of the most unusual is the quatrefoil-shaped Prentice Women's Hospital by Bertrand Goldberg. The blue-towered building (right) was the American Furniture Mart, a showroom center that has been converted to condominiums. The CBS studios are in a former riding club (far right).

Many wealthy families lived along Lake Shore Drive at the turn of the century. Their descendants live there now in the high rises that replaced the old mansions. Four remaining single-family homes can be seen – just barely – in the lower right where they have been rendered minuscule by their neighbors.

(Opposite) Landfill has become some of the city's most expensive and desirable real estate, the most notable example being this portion of the aptly named Gold Coast. At the center, facing Lake Shore Drive, are four glass-and-steel apartment buildings designed in the 1950s by Ludwig Mies van der Rohe. These buildings – along with the John Hancock Center shown right of center – set a standard of simplicity and sophistication which has not always been achieved by imitators who have built in the area.

Mansions still line North Lake Shore Drive in this photograph taken in 1937. The elegant Drake Hotel at the bend of the Drive was the work of society architects Marshall & Fox, and was completed in 1920. Benjamin Marshall reportedly attended to such minute details as the doormen's uniforms and the restaurant's recipes.

(Opposite) As Lake Shore Drive swings on a short east-west axis at the edge of downtown, it separates a wall of exclusive apartments and hotels from the not-so-exclusive Oak Street Beach. These buildings stood in glorious isolation through the 1920s. Then the thirty-seven-story Palmolive Building, shown standing immediately behind the Drake, intruded on their privacy when it was completed in 1929. Sadly, its rotating Lindbergh Beacon – named for the heroic aviator – no longer works. Its sweep of light would provide unwelcome illumination for offices and apartments in recent, taller buildings like the neighboring John Hancock Center which looms to the left.

The landfill that Grant Park rests on would be a rich study for archaeologists. Close to Michigan Avenue lies the debris from the Chicago Fire of 1871. Various layers for subsequent park expansions followed. In this 1930 view, the park's flatness contrasts with the city's growing skyline. Revisions in the building code in 1923 allowed taller buildings, provided they had setbacks. The Depression, however, put a stop to construction until the late 1950s, when the city embarked on another building boom. Shown opposite is Grant Park as it appears today.

(Opposite) The elevated train that rings the old central business district roughly defines the boundaries of what is called the Loop. Here, a group portrait of Chicago's architectural heritage serves as introduction and entry to the Loop. All but one of the Michigan Avenue buildings shown were erected before 1930, including the picturesque 1909 gothic high-rise clubhouse of the University Club at the center, and the turn-of-the-century Railway Exchange Building at the extreme left, where architect Daniel Burnham located his offices behind the round, top-story windows. According to folklore, Burnham arranged to have the low-rise home of the Chicago Symphony Orchestra placed to the north so the view from his office would not be obstructed. As with any group shot, taller subjects like the slope-sided First National Bank, and the Sears Tower — the world's tallest building — stand to the rear.

Despite its stone cladding and gothic detailing, the University Club (center) was technically up to date when it was erected in 1909. It was designed with a modern metal-supported structure by Holabird & Roche. Three buildings right of the club is a facade designed by Louis Sullivan. The pleasant Venetian facade of the 1893 Chicago Athletic Club stands to the right of Sullivan's.

(Opposite) Ornamental pylons and heroically scaled statues of equestrian Indians mark the beginning of Congress Street, a thoroughfare once envisioned as Chicago's premier boulevard and now, unfortunately, degraded to little more than an entry to the Eisenhower Expressway. To the right of the street stands the Auditorium Building, an 1890 architectural masterpiece designed by Adler & Sullivan that enfolds the incomparable Auditorium Theater. Next door, the ten-story Fine Arts Building has been a low-rent sanctuary for creative tenants for almost a century. The broad green roof of the Harold Washington library seems to hover overhead.

Between 1803-1857, Fort Dearborn stood on the south bank of the Chicago River at Michigan Avenue. Today, the Fort's outline is marked by plaques set in the pavement. The midwestern frontier is depicted on the 333 North Michigan Building, a 1928 skyscraper by Holabird & Root seen at the left. Across Michigan Avenue, the London Guarantee Building bends around an irregular lot at Wacker Drive. This curious skyscraper, topped with an adaptation of the Athenian Choragic Monument, was the work of Alfred S. Alschuler and was completed in 1923. Next door, the slender 1928 Mather Tower squeezes the maximum return from a small site.

Near where the gothic-looking Tribune Tower stands was the home of Chicago's first permanent settler, Jean Baptiste Point du Sable, a trader who lived there from roughly 1780-1796. The design by Hood and Howells for the Tribune Tower was first-place winner in a famous 1922 competition to design "the most beautiful building in the world." Across the street is the Wrigley Building, a terra-cotta confection by Graham, Anderson, Probst and White that was completed in 1924. To the left of Tribune Tower, the 1929 Medinah Athletic Club is now the Hotel Inter-Continental.

The 1920s song, "Chicago," launched State Street's reputation as "that great street." With its intersection at Madison touted as the "world's busiest corner," and as longtime home to department stores like Marshall Field's and Carson Pirie Scott, State Street's retailing supremacy seemed invincible. But in the past two decades, competition from Michigan Avenue and suburban malls has stolen some of State Street's thunder and much of its glamour. In a vain attempt to keep up, State was converted into a mall in 1979, explaining the odd meandering seen here. Realizing the error, city officials are now planning to "un-mall" it. One of Chicago's most important structures – the Reliance Building – is a modest presence in this image. It stands at the lower center and can be identified by the "Karolls" sign at its base. The Reliance was revolutionary when it was completed in 1895 after plans by D.H. Burnham & Company. With more window than wall area, the Reliance has a glassy appearance that anticipated skyscrapers to come.

By 1928, when this photograph was taken, the South Water Market that hugged the river's south bank had been replaced by Wacker Drive, a double-deck roadway with elegant promenades at the top, and a level for trucks and service vehicles below. Office towers sprang up as a result of the improvement. One example is the the domed terra-cotta Jeweler's Building, completed in 1926 and ingeniously designed to attract its targeted tenants. Jewelers – so the promotors said – could drive their cars straight into elevators that carried them directly to their office floors where they parked, thus reducing the opportunities for hold-ups. In this view, the north bank is still lined with lofts and warehouses. That was not to change for thirty years. The last of the old swing bridges, which pivoted in the middle to allow ships to pass, can be seen at Clark Street. It too is gone.

(Opposite) Movable double-leaf bridges carry the downtown streets across the Chicago River. In the past, traffic was endlessly knotted by bridges opened to allow mercantile ships to pass. Today, the main reason to raise the bridges is to let recreational sailboats out to lake moorings in the spring, and back to storage in the fall. All the bridges were once operated by full-time bridge tenders; now synchronized teams move from bridge to bridge by car, easily keeping ahead of the occasional boats and ships. Near the Kinsey Street bridge (bottom) a tunnel passing below the River was breached in April 1992. More than 250-million gallons of river water was delivered through the tunnel system to the sub-basements of many buildings, rising as high as thirty feet in some of them. Repair and cleanup went on for weeks.

Except for one clever imposter, the structures in this view of West Wacker Drive date from the 1920s. At the left, the 1929 LaSalle-Wacker Building is a classic setback composition of its period. Across the street is the 1927 Builders' Building, the design of which was carried into an adjoining 1986 addition that includes a sloping glass roof joining old with new. The Engineering Building and slender Chicago Evening Post Building are also from the late 1920s.

Showing not its photogenic curving facade but its more prosaic backside, the 333 West Wacker Drive building (left) stands in contrast to its next-door neighbor at 225 West Wacker Drive. The two were designed by Kohn Pedersen Fox of New York just six years apart and illustrate the firm's surprising change in style. Across the river is the Merchandise Mart, an architectural behemoth completed in 1930 by Marshall Field & Company, and purchased in 1946 by Joseph P. Kennedy, whose estate still owns the property. Known as the Mart, it houses textile and furniture showrooms.

(Opposite) Completed in 1983, the 333 West Wacker Building takes maximum advantage of a peculiar site formed by the bend in the Chicago River. The triangular lot was considered suitable only for parking until the New York architecture firm, Kohn Pedersen Fox designed a thirty-six-story office tower molded to the site. Facing the river with a curved skin of shimmering, reflective green glass, the building mirrors the light and seasons of the city.

Two skyscrapers dating from 1929 stand in an eternal face off across the South Branch of the Chicago River. The forty-five-story Civic Opera House combines offices with the home of the Lyric Opera, while the smaller Chicago Daily News Building was erected for one of the city's best — and sadly defunct — daily newspapers. Developers of both buildings probably envisioned the immediate replacement of the surrounding river warehouses with office towers like theirs, but more than forty years went by before further development occurred.

(Opposite) As urban legend has it, utilities magnate Samuel Insull had the Civic Opera House designed in the form of a giant throne facing away from downtown Chicago, allowing him to turn his back on the city that shunned him socially. In truth, Insull did quite well socially, and the chairlike form of the 1929 skyscraper is merely an efficient use of the site to create desirable rental offices that subsidized the 3,472-seat opera house tucked neatly under the seat.

In the late-nineteenth century, tall ships lined the South Branch of the Chicago River, moving cargo to and from the squat warehouses on the banks. Today, River traffic is largely confined to commuter boats, transporting cargoes of office workers to and from the tall buildings which now stand on the banks.

The play of light creates a photogenic syncopation on the curving glass walls of the 1987 Northwestern Atrium Center, a building combining a two-story commuter passenger station and a thirty-five-story office tower. Many would argue the building is no match for the turn-of-the-century granite railroad station that stood on the site previously.

The Morton International Building incorporates a feature rare for a building erected in 1991 —
an illuminated clock tower that follows in the best tradition of the Wrigley Building. Built on a
difficult site, the lower portion of the building had to be partially cantilevered over active railroad
tracks below. Following another Chicago tradition, the structure has been left out in the open
for all to see. Here, the cantilever supports are exposed on the roof.

The four buildings of Presidential Towers dominate an area west of downtown that was Chicago's skid row. Where there were once taverns, liquor stores and transient hotels; there are now shops, restaurants and a health club, serving a new middle-income clientele housed in 2,346 new apartments.

The thirty-four-story Richard J. Daley Center is an essay in elegant simplicity. It was completed in 1965 from a design by C.F. Murphy and Associates and contains offices and courtrooms. Half of the site is devoted to an open plaza, where the famous Chicago Picasso was unveiled in 1967. Within a short walk can be found similar plazas with works by Miro, Chagall, Calder, Dubuffet and Nevelson.

(Opposite) What book of urban aerial photography would be complete without a view of a highway interchange? The intersection of the Eisenhower and Dan Ryan expressways west of downtown is particularly choice for its photogenic laciness, and the road's penetration through an opening in the main Post Office.

In this city even a church can be a skyscraper as the twenty-one-story Chicago Temple demonstrates. Completed in 1923, the First Methodist Episcopal Church is located at ground level in a three-story sanctuary seating more than eight hundred people. Upper floors are rented to doctors, lawyers and other secular enterprises. A "sky chapel" – reputed to be the highest place of worship in the world – and the minister's quarters are in the upper spire. Once dominant on the skyline, the steeple's impact has been diminished by taller structures like the neighboring Brunswick Building, a distinguished essay in concrete completed in 1965.

(Opposite) Unlikely as it may seem at first glance, architect Helmut Jahn emulated the nineteenth-century courthouse in his 1985 design for the State of Illinois Chicago offices. But the building does have the traditional dome and rotunda, although abstracted into nearly unrecognizable forms by Jahn. Clad inside and out with turquoise, white, pink and clear glass, the building has confounded Chicagoans and visitors alike. Nevertheless, it acts as an architectural Pied Piper, attracting everyone to come look at it, even those who dismiss its design. The small free-form object in the corner of the plaza is a sculpture by Jean Dubuffet.

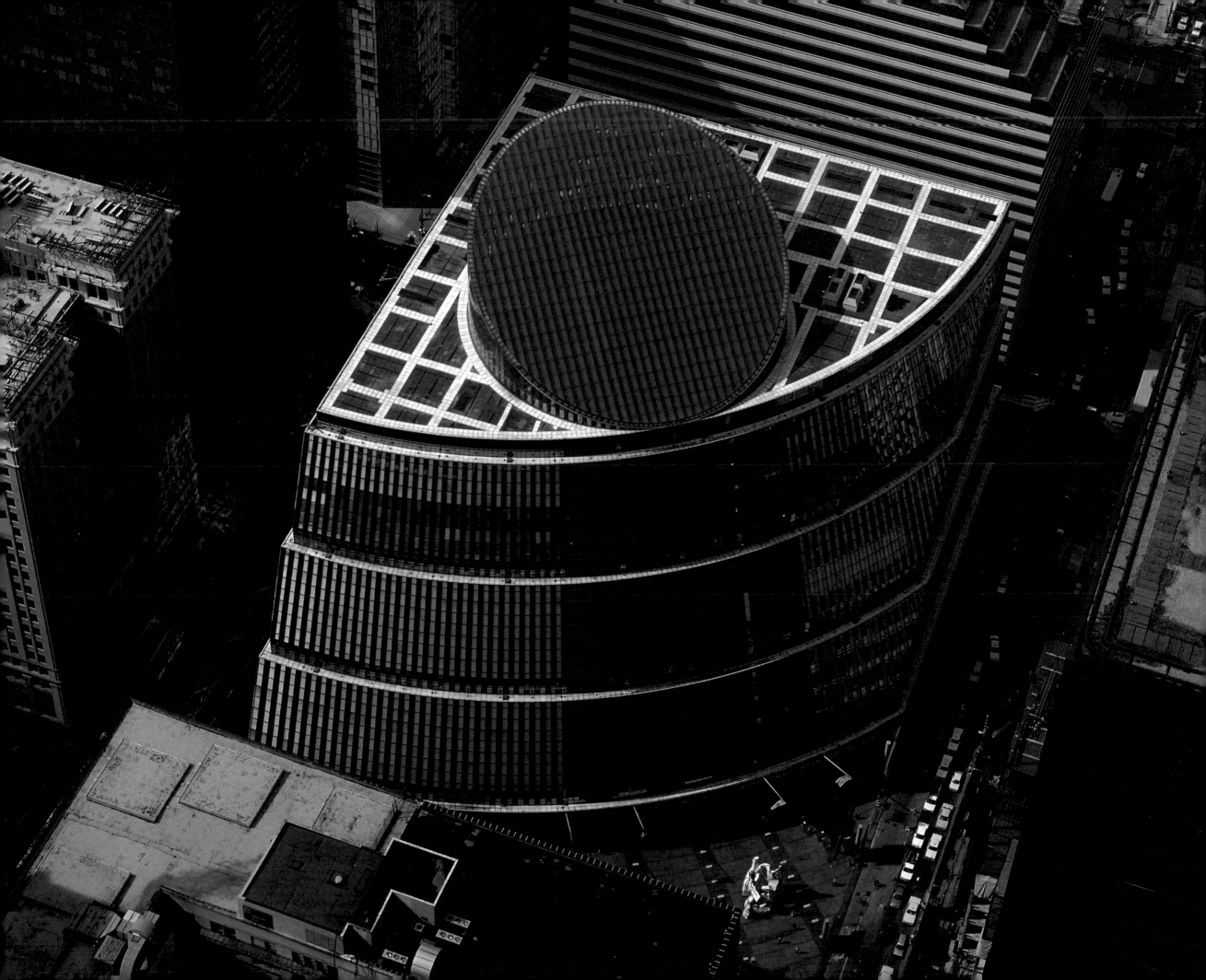

The Loop holds some of Chicago's oldest and most famous commercial buildings. For all their stature in the history books, many of them have been dwarfed by newer skyscrapers. Pilot Bob Kenney skillfully maneuvered his craft above the peaks to capture this view of the city center dominated by the sloping walls of the First National Bank Building and the slightly shorter Three First National Plaza to the left. Only the sharpest-eyed Chicagoan will pick out the Carson Pirie Scott Store, with its distinctive rounded corner just visible at the top left corner of Three First National. Completed in 1904 by master architect Louis H. Sullivan, Carson's stands at the corner of State and Madison, the base point for the city's address numbering system.

Finnish architect Eliel Saarinen's skyscraper design didn't win the Tribune Tower Competition of 1922, yet its influence on high rises continues. The most recent example is architect Cesar Pelli's 1991 stepped tower (left center) clad in granite, metal and glass at 181 West Madison Street.

Philip Johnson made reference to Chicago's past when he gave his 1980s design for the 190 South LaSalle office building an ornamental gabled top similar to Burnham & Root's 1892 Masonic Temple. The Masonic Temple was the tallest building in the world when it was completed. It rose to the then astounding height of twenty-one stories. Sadly, it was demolished in 1939.

An aerial perspective demystifies the powerful setbacks and soaring vertical detailing of the Chicago Board of Trade Building which stands at the foot of LaSalle Street in the heart of the financial district. This magnificent 1930 composition by

Holabird and Root remains an impressive part of the streetscape to everyone who sees it in the traditional manner, that is, from the ground. The abstract aluminum figure at the top is Ceres, the goddess of grain, by sculptor John Storrs. At night, the building's character is dramatized when it is bathed in brilliant floodlights.

(Opposite) Aerial perspective makes the buildings in this view look close together, but a dozen city blocks lie between the statue-topped Board of Trade Building at the bottom center, and the tall vertical shaft of the Amoco Building to the right. The latter has been captured in an embarrassing moment. Although less than twenty years old, deterioration required replacement of the building's original marble with a more durable granite. Scaffolds, where the stones were exchanged, are visible in this shot when the job was more than half finished. The flat-topped, forty-story Prudential Building to the left was Chicago's tallest in 1955 when it was completed. It has been surpassed many times, even by its needlelike annex completed in 1990.

Hammond, Beeby & Babka's winning design for the Harold Washington Library Center has renewed century-old arguments about appropriate architectural expression in Chicago. Completed in 1991, the library's heavy classical facades contrast with the surrounding turn-of-the-century Chicago School buildings. Ironically, it is the older buildings – pioneers in their time – that appear more modern. Two metal-framed buildings of skyscraper architect William Le Baron Jenney are visible, the 1891 Second Leiter Building to the right, and the 1890 Manhattan Building to the left. The bay windows of D.H. Burnham & Company's 1896 Fisher Building are visible opposite the library's left rear corner. Further left is the addition to the Monadnock Building by Holabird and Roche. At the upper left is Harry Weese and Associates triangular federal jail, completed in 1975.

Although the Michigan Avenue bridge had been open six years when this 1926 photo was taken, comparatively few developers had been enticed to build north of the Chicago River. The prominent exceptions are clearly visible: the Wrigley Building (left), Tribune Tower, (right) and the twenty-five-story Allerton Hotel completed in 1924 and shown midway down the street.

By 1931, when this view was shot, the northward migration had accelerated. The Allerton's prominence was usurped by the thirty-seven-story Palmolive Building at the far end of the street.

(Opposite) Ultimately the opening of the Michigan Avenue Bridge in 1920 transformed the area north of the river from a district of lofts and warehouses to an important business and shopping district. Pioneers in the area include the 1922 Wrigley Building with its gleaming white terra-cotta cladding and famous clock tower, and the picturesque, gothic-inspired 1925 Tribune Tower across the street. The development momentum has intensified in the past twenty years, giving stiff competition to the older central business district to the south.

Fifty acres of former rail yards and warehouses are being transformed as offices, hotels and condominiums are erected at Cityfront Center. The NBC Tower (center) looks older than it is. It was completed in 1989 in the style of the 1920s. On the right a survivor of the old days is partially visible. The turreted North Pier was a warehouse that has been converted to a shopping mall with apartments and offices in the upper stories. A travelling circus sets up on vacant Cityfront land in summer.

From 1892 until 1929, the Cook County Criminal Courts Building was witness to the tragic and macabre. Sausage manufacturer Adolph Luetgert stood trial here on charges that he ground up his wife in his plant's machinery, thus spoiling the city's appetite for sausages at the turn of the century. In 1924, the top floor courtroom was the stage for the Leopold and Loeb trial, at which Clarence Darrow made his impassioned plea against capital punishment. Found regularly in the fourth-floor pressroom were Ben Hecht, Charles MacArthur and Carl Sandburg. Life at the near-north-side courthouse was immortalized in Hecht and MacArthur's 1928 play, *The Front Page*. Since it was converted to offices, the building has become the scene for adventures in enterprise.

The twin residential towers of Marina City have been an icon of the city since their completion in 1964, but their significance is more than purely visual. Built amidst the grimy warehouses that once lined the north bank of the Chicago River, they are a part of the first multi-use residential complex built downtown. Because of Marina City's initial isolation and the lack of stores and services, architect Bertrand Goldberg invented a self-contained living environment. The complex included a skating rink, bowling alley, marina, shops, movie theaters and an office building. As this current view shows, the site is no longer isolated. The IBM Building stands on the left, and the Hotel Nikko to the right.

The block of trees in the foreground marks Washington Square, one of the city's oldest public parks. It is also called "Bughouse Square," an appellation won during the first half of the twentieth century when the park was the site of frequent impromptu soapbox orations. Speeches here are rare today, but the park's reputation and nickname hold firm. The Newberry Library, a major research institution, stands soberly to the left, while picturesque late-nineteenth-century buildings add character to the park's eastern perimeter.

The Water Tower's survival of the Chicago Fire of 1871 is no less remarkable than its escape from later demolition. Over the years, road-widening projects requiring the Tower's destruction have been proposed. Fortunately, the Water Tower's popularity as an eccentric memento of the Fire has permanently scotched those plans. Completed in 1869 as part of the city's water works, the Water Tower's castled stone facade is merely a romantic casing for a prosaic, and now inactive, iron standpipe.

The gracious old houses and apartments of the near-north-side Gold Coast attract all sorts of residents, sometimes in unlikely combinations. Three blocks separate the former Playboy Mansion from the Catholic Archbishop of Chicago's home (top). (The Playboy Mansion is the building with three dormers in the photograph on the right.) Hugh Hefner left the Playboy Mansion for California, giving the house — complete with basement grotto pool — to the Art Institute. Renamed Hefner Hall, it has become a dormitory for art students. In the meantime, the Catholic hierarchy has remained unshakably ensconced down the street.

The Chicago Historical Society (center) at Clark Street and North Avenue marks the beginning of Lincoln Park's more than twelve-hundred-acre expanse north along the lakefront. The portion pictured was the city cemetery until the mid-nineteenth century when all the marked graves were relocated. One immovable mausoleum was left just north of the museum, and routine excavations occasionally unearth unidentified human remains. The rounded structure in the foreground is the four-thousand-seat Moody Memorial Church, erected in 1926 for a congregation established by nineteenth-century spellbinder evangelist Dwight L. Moody.

(Opposite) A farm in the city? The Lincoln Park Zoo is one of the city's most popular attractions, including among its exhibits a model farm complete with cows, horses, and sheep. Cafe Brauer, a beautifully restored 1907 restaurant and public refectory stands immediately above the farm, identified by its tile roof and circular drive. With its exotic palms and orchids, the Lincoln Park Conservatory – shown in the upper center – is a particularly welcome refuge in the winter for cold-weary Chicagoans.

The public housing project, Cabrini-Green, stands where a tough immigrant neighborhood called Little Hell did early in the twentieth century. Cabrini started out well. In 1941 the Chicago Housing Authority replaced sixteen acres of deteriorating tenements with modern apartments in pleasant two- and three-story buildings. But changing policy at the Authority called for high rises when Cabrini was expanded in 1958 and again in 1962. Little Hell was effectively rebuilt. Cabrini is now an unmanageable sea of towers with little apparent sense of community among its residents. High-priced real estate looms on all sides causing speculation about Cabrini's fate.

(Opposite) The massive warehouses of Montgomery Ward & Company follow exactly the shore of the Chicago River, which long served to transport goods to and from the buildings. With its famous mail-order catalogue a thing of the past, the near-north-side buildings have been largely converted to offices, supplementing the firm's later high-rise administration building to the right. On the opposite side of the River is the printing plant of the Chicago Tribune where newspaper copy is received by microwave from the Tribune Tower on Michigan Avenue.

This is the countenance of hard-core industry. Located northwest of downtown, Goose Island was formed by a channel dug in the mid-nineteenth century that straightened a bend in the North Branch of the Chicago River. Geese kept by Irish immigrants who lived there reputedly gave the island its name. By the time this 1933 view was shot, residents and their birds had departed making way for the industries that cover the island. The tall, round object to the right is a gas storage tank, a once familiar, now extinct feature of the urban landscape.

(Opposite) Heavy industry still dominates Goose Island despite the hungry gaze of developers who imagine its buildings transformed into high-ceilinged residential lofts. Legislation has kept speculators at bay, saving this area for the city's diminished industrial base.

When Polish immigrants built their church on the Northwest Side they recreated a piece of the old country. The design for St. Stanislaus Kostka Church is based on a church in Krakow. Since it was completed in 1881, St. Stanislaus has towered over the homes and workplaces of its parishioners and served generations of Chicago's Poles. In the 1950s, to avoid offending the powerful Polish constituency, city officials bent the Northwest Expressway around the church – which stood square in the highway's path. Today, Spanish as well as Polish is spoken here.

Within distant view of St. Stanislaus stands another of Chicago's grand old Polish Catholic churches, St. Mary of the Angels, which was completed in 1920. Citing shrinking attendance and costly repairs – including catching the falling terra-cotta angels – the Archdiocese sought to close this church. Salvation came from the congregation and its vigorous fund-raising campaign.

In the late-nineteenth and early-twentieth centuries, most of Chicago's neighborhoods had small commercial districts reflecting the residents' cultures. The Polish and Eastern European community was centered at the intersection of Milwaukee, Damen and North Avenues where the twelve-story Northwest Tower, stands as testament to the neighborhood's early prosperity. Now a multi-cultural economy animates this lively intersection despite competition from outlying shopping centers.

Holy Trinity Orthodox Cathedral is unusual among the works of architect Louis H. Sullivan. The church was completed in 1903 for a northwest-side Russian congregation initially established in Chicago using funds given by Czar Nicholas II. Congregation members, who originally lived in the area, have dispersed. Now they come from all over Chicago for Sunday services.

Humboldt Park, on the Near Northwest Side, is one of many large parks strategically sited through the city and connected by broad grassy boulevards. They were laid out in the latter half of the nineteenth century and developed over succeeding years by master landscape planners like Frederick Law Olmsted, Jens Jensen and Alfred Caldwell. Architect William Le Baron Jenney, who is known more for developing the skyscraper than designing parks, contributed much of Humboldt Park's plan. At the turn of the century Jens Jensen reshaped the park according to his vision of the urban prairie.

(Opposite) Talented landscape designers have shaped Graceland Cemetery making it one of the country's most beautiful urban cemeteries. Since it was established in 1861, Graceland has been the burial place for many of the city's most prominent families. Elaborate and costly monuments bear names like Field, Pullman, Palmer and McCormick. Also buried here are some of the city's greatest architects, Louis Sullivan, John Root and Ludwig Mies van der Rohe, among them. Many of the monuments are significant works by important nineteenth- and twentieth-century architects and sculptors. While Graceland's residents rest peacefully, a string of yellow school buses parked outside the walls wait to pick up their passengers after the Cubs game.

The north-side campus of DePaul University is a pleasing combination of old and new structures within tree-lined grounds. Largely because of the University the surrounding neighborhood is remarkably stable, making the phrase "DePaul area" a valuable asset in real estate ads.

(Opposite) Whether the Chicago Cubs win or not, being in Wrigley Field is a pleasure. Wrigley is one of the oldest major-league ballparks in the country, and it has a quirky, archaic charm, with its ivy-covered outfield walls and manual scoreboard. Wrigley was the last in the majors to install lights for night games, finally succumbing in 1988. There were protests by traditionalists, who oppose lights on principle, and some residents, who feared losing their evening serenity to inebriated fans. Of course, many "Wrigleyville" residents are fans themselves as the elaborate viewing decks erected on the surrounding rooftops demonstrate.

In 1928 luxury apartments and hotels hugged the lakeshore south of Bryn Mawr Avenue. The massive Edgewater Beach Apartments are shown in the left foreground and the two Edgewater Beach Hotel buildings with their distinctive cupolas are seen in the center.

(Opposite) The view is greatly altered by 1991. Extensive landfill made room for Lincoln Park and the expansion of North Lake Shore Drive. The Edgewater Beach Apartments still stand, although much further inland. Unfortunately, losing its lake frontage proved fatal to the Edgewater Beach Hotel. It was demolished in 1969 and was replaced by the bland black high rise at the center.

Chicago's boating scene is democratic. The city's marinas — including Diversey Harbor pictured here — are maintained and operated by the Chicago Park District and sailing dinghies float alongside fifty-foot ocean racers. Suburbanites might feel like second-class citizens. Anyone who doesn't live in the city proper pays more for their slip.

The northern end of Belmont Harbor is popular with fishermen who can be seen there in warm months teasing fat fish out of the water with some careful rod and line work.

Belmont Harbor is discretely sheltered from view by its protective land mass extending into the lake.

For those foolhardy enough to enroll in it, the Frostbite Fleet sails dinghy races in Montrose Harbor through the winter months.

The park around Montrose Harbor is ideal for back-seat sailors monitoring the skills of skippers out on the lake.

(Opposite) From a practical standpoint, star moorings at Montrose Harbor are an efficient use of precious space. From an aesthetic standpoint, they make an irresistible subject for the aerial photographer.

In 1906 the Jesuit Order purchased a tract of lakefront land in far-north Rogers Park which ultimately became Loyola University. The beautiful site has some disadvantages, like the constant maintenance of sea walls to prevent the lake from claiming the campus as its own.

(Opposite) When Rosehill Cemetery was established in 1859 it was so remote from the city that funeral parties arrived by specially chartered trains. Rosehill was subsequently enveloped by the expanding city and absorbed into the city's Far North Side. The huge mausoleum is a labyrinth of private and family burial chambers with a capacity exceeding the population of many small towns.

The Century of Progress Exposition of 1933-1934 provided respite from the Depression. Visitors who made their way to Chicago in battered autos gazed admiringly at the glass tower of the Nash Exhibit, the wonders of the cable-suspended Transportation Building, and the Chrysler Motors exhibit. Here an early Goodyear blimp comes in for a landing, dropping a line to the waiting ground crew.

(Opposite) The broad roof of McCormick Place gives Chicago's 1971 convention center a dramatic presence on its lakefront site and affirms the city's jealously guarded reputation as a major convention center. An annex completed in 1986 across Lake Shore Drive conveys a different architectural feeling altogether, with its roof supported by cables hung from projecting masts.

Proximity is the draw at Dearborn Park. Residents of this community find their downtown offices within easy walking distance of home. The apartments and townhouses were constructed on former railyards immediately south of the Loop and were intended for middle-class residents.

(Opposite) These commuter railyards on the river south of downtown recall what much of Chicago looked like when it was a rail center. The Chicago area is still important to shipping, but freight facilities that occupied premium downtown land have been moved to outlying areas where property values are not as high.

After a municipal crackdown on the notorious "Old Levee" early in the century, vice lords and their crooked operations moved out, and enterprising Chinese businessmen moved in. Chinatown was born. Since then the area around Wentworth Avenue and Cermak Road on the South Side has been transformed to reflect its residents' native land and culture. Chinatown continues to expand as families grow and newcomers arrive. Developers from the community are building shops and housing on the vacant land seen in the distance.

(Opposite) The distinctive clock tower of Dearborn Station stands amid buildings which housed printers until recently. Changing technologies and rising real estate values forced printers to move to the suburbs and Printing House Row now refers to an enclave of loft apartments, shops and restaurants. For that matter, no trains arrive at Dearborn Station any longer. It has been remodeled as offices, a music school and stores. The park and newer buildings in the foreground are part of Dearborn Park, a housing development designed to attract middle-class residents to downtown addresses.

The Henry B. Clarke house has miraculously eluded natural disasters and wrecking balls to become Chicago's oldest building. It was erected in 1837 in a country setting that has since become the Near South Side. When the house was restored it was moved to a lot adjacent to Prairie Avenue, where late-nineteenth-century millionaires lived on "the sunny street that held the sifted few." To the left, the inner courtyard of the John J. Glessner House can be seen, one of the last works of architect H.H. Richardson before his death in 1886. The 1891 French chateau of piano and organ manufacturer W.W. Kimball is visible at the upper left.

(Opposite) When Bertrand Goldberg submitted the scheme for this public housing project in the early 1960s, hesitant federal officials complained the design was "too good" for its intended low-income residents. The Raymond Hilliard Center was deliberately planned to encourage interaction between senior citizens, housed in twin circular buildings, and families with children, residing in adjacent semi-circular structures. The resulting ensemble is one of Chicago's more successful public housing projects. The site was once the center of Chicago's notorious turn-of-the-century red light district. The sumptuously decorated Everleigh Club, which catered to the elite, was one of the brothels that stood here.

Opened in 1892 as a luxury hotel catering to world's fair visitors, the Lexington Hotel later achieved a more sinister reputation as headquarters for Alphonse "Scarface" Capone. From 1928-1931, Capone ruled the dark side of Prohibition-era Chicago from a corner office on the fourth floor. Visitors who penetrated his fortified sanctum said three portraits hung on Capone's office wall – George Washington, Abraham Lincoln and Chicago Mayor "Big Bill" Thompson. Only one of these gentlemen was on the take. Convicted of tax evasion in 1931, Capone's career was over by the time he was thirty-two. Despite the Lexington's excellent south-side location near the convention center, the hotel has been awaiting rehabilitation for over a decade.

Although far from scenes of battle, Chicago has historic Civil War-era sites. The tomb of Lincoln's political opponent, Stephen A. Douglas, stands at Thirty-fifth Street near Lake Shore Drive where his country estate – now swallowed by the city – once did. In the foreground is the former Soldiers' Home where injured soldiers recuperated within sight of Lake Michigan and touched by its cool breezes. In the distance is the former site of Camp Douglas, a prisoner-of-war camp where over four-thousand Confederate soldiers died from disease. At one time, prisoners conspired to overrun the camp and seize Chicago in the name of the Confederacy.

(Opposite) The initial campus plan and many of the major buildings of the Illinois Institute of Technology were designed by noted German architect Ludwig Mies van der Rohe, who moved to Chicago in 1938 to chair the school's architecture department. The two older red-brick buildings date from the school's beginning in the late-nineteenth century as the Armour Institute of Technology.

A two-mile wall of buildings comes into view on the Dan Ryan Expressway at Garfield Boulevard. These are the Robert Taylor Homes. Started in 1960, they are a textbook example of a discredited approach to housing low-income families.

(Opposite) Hardly a word of protest was heard when replacement was proposed for Comiskey Park, the home of the Chicago White Sox since 1910. When the new Comiskey opened for the season in 1991, most fans lined up for tickets. The more sentimentally inclined paid twenty dollars for an "official" brick from the now-demolished park.

The Union Stock Yards represented different things over the 106 years they were in operation between 1865-1971. The city's reputation as a commercial center was in part secured by meat-packing companies with names like Swift and Armour that were clustered around the Yards. To immigrant families, the stockyards meant employment. To Upton Sinclair, the Yards symbolized unfair and unsanitary working conditions which he exposed in his turn-of-the-century book, *The Jungle*. The view above shows the stockyards rebuilt after a fire in 1934. The International Amphitheater is in the center foreground, adjoined on the right to the now-demolished Stock Yards Inn. Further right is a replica of Independence Hall that was the Livestock National Bank. The Amphitheater and Bank survive in the contemporary view (right). But most of the stockyards have become an industrial park. Long gone are the days when acres and acres of live animals made winds from the south painfully aromatic. The original limestone entry gate, seen on a traffic island at the far right, has been preserved as a memento of the Stock Yards.

In 1891 the University of Chicago emerged from the unlikely mix of oil and dry goods. Land in the south-side neighborhood of Hyde Park was donated for the campus by State Street merchant Marshall Field and early funding for the school came from Standard Oil baron John D. Rockefeller. The purity of the "collegiate gothic" architecture is shown unspoiled in this 1931 view. One of the most prominent structures on campus is the misnamed Rockefeller Chapel (bottom center). It is really a twentieth-century cathedral with a vast and soaring interior. It was completed in 1928 and was designed by a master of the genre, Bertram Grosvenor Goodhue. The grandstands of Stagg Field, visible in the distance, were demolished long ago.

(Opposite) The University of Chicago grew up beside the Midway Plaisance, a landscaped thoroughfare connecting Jackson Park, to the east, with Washington Park, to the west. During the World's Columbian Exposition of 1893, sideshows – including the world's first ferris wheel and "Little Egypt" – were on the Midway. The University left gothic revival behind in the 1950s; both Eero Saarinen and Ludwig Mies van der Rohe completed commissions for the school.

In his colossal sculpture, Fountain of Time, Lorado Taft interpreted two lines from a poem by Austin Dobson:

Time goes you say. Ah no,
Alas time stays, we go.

The concrete sculpture marks the entry to Washington Park. It took fourteen years to complete, and was dedicated in 1922. Among those portrayed passing the shrouded figure of Time is the sculptor who is depicted on the rear elevation.

A twelve-foot bronze by Henry Moore marks the place where the first self-sustained controlled nuclear reaction occurred on December 2, 1942. Dedicated twenty-five years later, the sculpture suggests both a mushroom cloud and a human skull, fitting images to mark an event called, "the beginning of the end" by some. The experiment by University of Chicago scientists was conducted under the stands of the now-demolished Stagg Field football stadium.

Aerial photography reveals the unity of form and plan in Frank Lloyd Wright's Robie House, completed in 1910 in Hyde Park. The asymmetric multi-level form freely expresses the interior. The upper level contains bedrooms with broad roof overhangs sheltering windows facing in all directions. The living and dining rooms are elevated above the street and are divided by a central fireplace and staircase rather than enclosing walls. The house is now occupied by the offices of the University of Chicago Alumni Association.

(Opposite) Even though it was the only major surviving structure of the 1893 World's Columbian Exposition, this building seemed destined for neglect. After the fair, it was occupied and then abandoned by the Field Museum and stood vacant for more than ten years. It was finally rescued in the 1930s by the Museum of Science and Industry which remains in it today. The building's original stucco has been removed and replaced with a more durable stone and terra-cotta cladding. The museum's eclectic collection includes a captured World War II German Submarine (right of the main building). A 1986 domed addition (extreme right) contains space exhibits and an Omnivision theater. Elegant little Promontory Park juts into the lake at the right.

Silent cannons and a forty-foot granite monument mark the mass grave of more than four-thousand Confederate soldiers who died while imprisoned at Camp Douglas. Located at Oak Woods Cemetery on the South Side, the plot was purchased by the federal government in 1867. The monument was dedicated by President Grover Cleveland on Memorial Day, 1895.

The New Regal Theater takes its name and inspiration from the legendary Regal Theater at Forty-seventh and King Drive. Until its closing and eventual demolition in 1973, the old Regal was the showcase for black performing arts in the city. The New Regal opened on the far South Side in 1987 in an old fantasy Moorish movie palace by architect John Eberson. The wall facing the parking lot has a mural depicting the original Regal and its performers.

(Opposite) The Pullman community is a curious artifact of American industrial history. In 1880 rail-car magnate George Pullman established what he hoped would be an uplifting, self-sufficient company town thirteen miles south of downtown Chicago. It contained — on impeccably maintained grounds — the Pullman Palace Car Company factories, a hotel, rental housing for the workers, a market, and a school. Despite the utopian pretensions, workers felt the town was more controlled than ideal. Indeed, the town was a contentious issue during the Pullman Strike of 1894. While workers' salaries had been lowered, rents had not. Eventually, the courts ruled Pullman could not own and manage the town, and the buildings were sold to individuals. The Hotel Florence can be seen immediately above the landscaped park (center left), and the curving buildings of Market Square are to the right.

Located on the south edge of the city, the Illinois International Port reaffirms Chicago's reputation as a world trade center. Ships from around the world enter Lake Michigan via the Saint Lawrence Seaway to pick up grain and other cargo. Grain elevators like these are descendants of the structures that crowded the banks of the Chicago River in the nineteenth century, but which have been replaced by office towers.

(Opposite) Despite tough times, steel-making operations continue just over the state line at Inland Steel's expansive East Chicago, Indiana plant. International freighters pick up and discharge cargo on one side of the plant while pleasure boats dock serenely on the other.

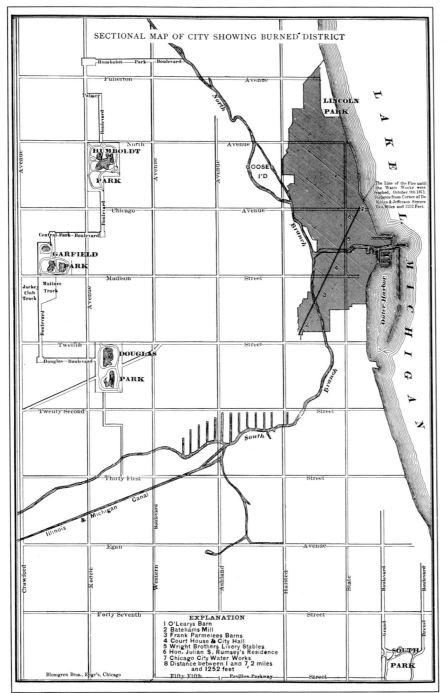

SECTIONAL MAP OF CITY SHOWING BURNED DISTRICT

EXPLANATION
1 O'Learys Barn
2 Batehams Mill
3 Frank Parmelees Barns
4 Court House & City Hall
5 Wright Brothers Livery Stables
6 Hon. Julian S. Rumsey's Residence
7 Chicago City Water Works
8 Distance between 1 and 7, 2 miles
and 1252 feet

Blomgren Bros., Engr's, Chicago

The Great Chicago Fire of 1871 began in the O'Leary barn on the West Side. Swept northeast by high winds, the Fire devoured more than three square miles of the city center, killed over 300 people, and left 90,000 homeless. The true story of how the wood barn caught fire will probably never be known, legends about the cow that kicked the lantern notwithstanding. Strangely, the

O'Leary cottage survived the Fire. The training school for Chicago firefighters (above) stands where the Great Fire began. The bright orange walls of the Chicago Fire Academy are a fitting backdrop for a thirty-foot commemorative bronze of leaping flames by Egon Weiner.

(Opposite) The Chicago Stadium, which appears as a desolate island amid empty parking lots, is transformed when the Chicago Bulls basketball team or the Chicago Blackhawks hockey team play. Aside from sports events, the west-side stadium has been the stage for national political conventions, rock concerts, ice shows and more. But the 1929 building is likely to be gone soon, plans are underway for replacing it with a new facility.

Erection of the University of Illinois campus required partial demolition of a residential neighborhood. Spared from destruction were the original house and dining hall of Hull House, the settlement house established by Jane Addams and Ellen Gates Starr in 1889. Although dwarfed by campus buildings, their rooftops can be seen at right center.

The near-southwest campus of the University of Illinois at Chicago is the work of Walter Netsch of Skidmore, Owings & Merrill. The campus plan and buildings make a dizzying environment of changing spaces, levels and materials. A good example is seen in the abstract forms of the Science and Engineering Building (center) from which a concrete ramp extends to the rectangular Science and Engineering Laboratories.

When it was established in the nineteenth century, Cook County Hospital was far outside the city. As the city grew the hospital was enveloped. Now this near-west-side area is a major medical center complex shared by several institutions.

THE SUBURBS

The Evanston shorefront has been largely taken up by Northwestern University since the school's founding in 1851. As shown in this juxtaposition of historic and contemporary shots, the character of the campus has changed. Visible in both views, however, is the 1870 University Hall with its picturesque steeple — now the oldest building on campus (left of center in both photographs). A more current landmark is the 1966 Lindheimer Astronomical Research Center which stands on Lake Michigan landfill (opposite, upper right).

Evanston began in the mid-nineteenth century as a self-sufficient village separated from Chicago by miles of sparsely settled land. As Chicago grew Evanston was ultimately demoted to suburb. But, with a population of 73,233, an impressive downtown, and prestigious Northwestern University within its boundaries, Evanston maintains its independence. Its reputation for primness is also intact. To protect Northwestern students from evil influences, legislation forbidding liquor sales in Evanston remained in place for more than a century. The regulation has been relaxed, but Evanston — still home to the Woman's Christian Temperance Union — remembers its teetotaler past.

One-hundred-acre Calvary Cemetery is in Evanston, just beyond the Chicago city limits. Many of the bodies originally buried in Chicago's old Catholic Cemetery on the lakefront near downtown were reinterred at Calvary in the mid-nineteenth century.

The glistening profile of the Baha'i House of Worship is visible for miles from the air. Its commanding lakefront site in Wilmette was selected for the national temple as interest in the religion spread in the United States early in the 1900s. Architect Louis Bourgeois, himself a Ba'hai follower, designed the building. The cornerstone was laid in 1921 but Bourgeois, who died in 1930, did not live to see the temple finished. The building was not completed until 1953. The 1930s view shows the structure before its lacy concrete dome cladding was installed. A quartz aggregate mixed into the concrete makes the building sparkle in sunlight. The lakefront mansion (far left, above) was architect Benjamin H. Marshall's. The quintessential hedonist millionaire, Marshall's estate included a tropical garden with a glass roof which could be opened for parties, a dining-room table which rose from the floor at the flick of a switch and a nautical bar that rocked on hydraulic lifts.

The delicate petal-like forms of architect Minoru Yamasaki's 1964 synagogue have been forever violated by the stark geometric additions to the front and either side. Now the best view of the Temple of North Shore Congregation Israel in Glencoe is from the beach.

(Opposite) When this strip was still unincorporated it was called "No Man's Land" and was home to nightclubs and speakeasies visited by crowds from Chicago and the suburbs. The surreptitious delights have gone, and this tract is now known as the border between Wilmette and Kenilworth. The high-rise residential buildings that mark this edge are unusual. These north-shore suburbs are characterized by luxurious single-family homes. Shops and offices occupy the Spanish-style buildings in Plaza Del Lago (center left).

The Lake Shore Country Club in Glencoe peacefully co-exists with the high-priced residential real estate of Chicago's suburban North Shore. Outside potential hazards from wayward golf balls, clubs like this are considered model neighbors by nearby residents.

These Highland Park houses are quite secluded. They are set far back from well-travelled thoroughfares.

The regional offices of Ameritech in Hoffman Estates follow the suburban corporate model; low and rambling, these buildings cover a lot of ground and contain as much floor area as many downtown skyscrapers.

(Opposite) Lake Forest had lakefront property but no beach to speak of until the suburbs created one in the late 1980s with a series of erosion-resistant bulwarks.

Starting early in the century as a private amusement park in Highland Park, Ravinia Park has become a summertime show-case for concerts and performances. Some concert goers choose to sit in the grass and set out elaborate gourmet picnics served with fine china, silver and linens. State-of-the-art facilities have altered the park's early rustic charm, but the quality of the performances continues to make events memorable.

(Opposite) The lakes and grounds of the Botanic Garden look as though they have always been there. In fact, they were hewn out of three hundred acres in Glencoe fairly recently. The main building, shown here, was designed by Edward Larrabee Barnes and completed in 1976. Barnes used understated natural materials and horizontal planes to make the building appear to be a part of the landscape. It houses a large exhibition space, secluded courtyards and greenhouses. Changing exhibits, educational programs and thematic plantings make the Botanic Gardens a popular weekend destination.

(Opposite) The commuter rail line provides fast access from Lake Forest to Chicago. Some of the wealthiest and most influential people in Illinois have ridden that line, working in Chicago while living in Lake Forest's wooded setting. Veteran residents of the exclusive community were aroused a few years ago when television heavy Mr. T purchased the Armour estate and cut down most of the trees on the property. The barren tract to the left is now the T estate. Mr. T said allergies were the reason for the deforestation.

Fort Sheridan seems more like an impeccably maintained estate than an army base. It stands on a 725-acre wooded site in Highwood overlooking Lake Michigan. Attractive Romanesque-style buildings, including the tall water tower in the center, date from the Fort's founding in the 1890s and are the work of the Chicago architectural firm, Holabird & Roche. Since is was scheduled for closing, the Fort has been covetously eyed for new uses.

Lake Forest's Market Square offers a largely unheeded lesson on how an automobile-dependent shopping center can become an amenity. In contrast to the usual slab of asphalt, the picturesque, eclectically detailed buildings of Market Square are set back from the main street with shops surrounding a landscaped square. Architect Howard Van Doren Shaw designed the square which was erected between 1912-1917.

The Kemper Insurance Company in northwest Long Grove has its own golf course. The view of the course from company windows is undoubtedly a strong deterrent to playing unauthorized games on company time.

Shopping malls turn traditional retailing inside out. Stores once lured shoppers from the street with eye-catching window displays. But malls turn inward, leaving blank facades and acres of parking out on the street. Developments like Woodfield Mall in northwest suburban Schaumburg are strategically positioned to draw patrons from a large radius, giving tough competition to surviving "Main Streets" in surrounding communities.

The first restaurant in the McDonald's chain opened in 1955 in Des Plaines and was later rebuilt as a museum by the corporation (upper right). The passage of time has given the original golden arches, developed in 1952 by architects Stanley Meston and Charles W. Fish, a degree of integrity, particularly when compared to the mansard-roof version (bottom).

Like many other corporations, Sears is moving from downtown to seek its fortunes in reduced tax rates in the suburbs. Some corporate offices will remain in Sears Tower, justifying keeping the company name on the world's tallest building. Sears' vast new headquarters in Hoffman Estates cover 788 acres, the building alone takes 120 acres. A total of 5,700 people will work here when the building is completed late in 1992.

(Opposite) The Shriners' architecture is every bit as fanciful as their red fez hats and secret handshakes. For evidence, examine the exotic Moorish-influenced 1920s clubhouse at the Medinah Country Club in the northwest suburbs.

As it makes its unhurried way, this paddle wheeler emphasizes the Fox River Valley's picturesque qualities. Looking south, the communities of far west suburban Geneva and Saint Charles are visible in the distance.

(Below) Forty miles away is distance enough to challenge the word suburb. So it is the City of Aurora. Incorporated in 1857, Aurora united two rival communities on opposite banks of the Fox River. To appease both, the city center was put in the middle, on Stolp Island. The city's nineteenth-century economy was animated by rail traffic; the old roundhouse seen in the distance which was rehabilitated as shops is a reminder of that era. Nearby expressways stimulated a recent economic boom by making Aurora a sought-after site for corporate development.

(Opposite) The underground ring of the collider at Fermi National Accelerator Laboratory is plainly visible from the air. Sub-atomic matter is the chief subject of study here. Nuclear particles, sped along by magnetic forces, circle the ring until they approach the speed of light. In hopes of observing the still-unseen quark, scientists study the sub-particles that occur when particles collide. The 6,800-acre lab grounds are the scene for demonstrations in wildlife and ecology conservation. Indigenous prairie grasses have been restored on the six-hundred acres lying within the ring and a buffalo herd wanders a preserve.

This large yard in Joliet — so similar to others scattered throughout the region — demonstrates the important role railroads played in the development of Chicago and outlying communities. Cargo cars are lined up like beads on a wire to the left. Locomotives, however, are kept in stalls in the roundhouse on the right.

Decades after gravel was extracted from its deep pits, this quarry near Plainfield has been transformed into a private sportsmens' club. Flooding has returned the site to an approximation of its natural state and provided the ideal environment for hunting and fishing.

Ever since the mayor said she saw four Ns on this building its been called the "N Building." It has become an emblem for suburban Naperville, where it stands. It was designed by Chicago architect Helmut Jahn, who is mum on whether the Ns were intentional.

Argonne National Laboratory sprawls over 1,700 acres twenty-five miles southwest of Chicago. Work at Argonne is focused on applications of nuclear energy. The first nuclear reactor to produce electricity was designed and built here and other advanced reactors are being developed. The Laboratory was begun with government funding after World War II in hopes of advancing historic scientific work done during the War.

(Opposite) People who live here would rather be flying. Brookeridge Aero Estates is a residential airport with 120 homes and about one hundred planes used for recreation and commuting. Streets are wide enough to accommodate taxiing aircraft. Many of the planes are restored classics and there are even some homemade models.

The Chicago Golf Club in Wheaton has the oldest eighteen-hole course in the country. The private club was founded in 1892 by Charles Blair McDonald, a slicer who designed a course he could play on – mostly dog-legs to the right.

(Opposite) By the early 1900s the unabated expansion of Chicago and its suburbs threatened to devour what was left in the metropolitan area of the natural landscape. Legislation set aside land for protected forests that would counterbalance the built environment. The dividends are colorfully evident in this autumn view of the Palos Forest Preserve at the south end of the metropolitan area.

Much of the concrete and gravel used in building Chicago came from the massive limestone quarries in suburban Thornton. The constant expansion of the quarry — said to be the largest of its kind in the world — has left surface roads balanced on thin slivers of stone.

(Opposite) All eighteen fairways are visible in this view of Olympia Fields.

In 1990, Stateville Correctional Center in Joliet was home to roughly 2,049 inmates, exceeding its intended capacity by about one third. When it opened in 1925 Stateville housed first-time offenders who worked the grounds of the surrounding State Penitentiary Farm. Today it is a maximum-security prison and prisoners who go outside the walls are frowned upon.

Brookfield Zoo is one of the finest urban zoos in the country. Since its opening in 1934, the zoo, located in west suburban Brookfield, has expanded and upgraded several times to meet contemporary standards and technologies. It is now an impressive two-hundred-acre facility simulating a range of natural environments.

In 1868, Frederick Law Olmsted developed an influential plan that transformed a scrubby tract on the banks of the Des Plaines River into the idyllic suburban community, Riverside. Olmsted planned Riverside with generous lots plotted along meandering tree-lined thoroughfares, following the River's gentle bends.

An architectural revolution took place in this building. This was where Frank Lloyd Wright lived and worked for many years, designing buildings that influenced architecture internationally. The tall angled roof marks the family quarters. The low adjoining structure was Wright's studio, added in 1898. The geometric shapes define the internal functions, the large octagon marks the drafting room, and the smaller skylit octagon opposite is a library. The entire complex has been restored and opened to the public.

Frank Lloyd Wright's Unitarian Church in Oak Park is one of the seminal works of twentieth-century design. The sanctuary is located in the cube to the left and is adjoined to the smaller community house on the right. Windows in the sanctuary were minimized to screen out noise, but abundant light comes through a large skylight. The entire building represents an early use of reinforced concrete construction.

EVENTS

Less than eight years after the Wright Brothers' first powered flight, Chicagoans became acquainted with the airplane at the 1911 International Aviation Meet in Grant Park. Several hundred thousand spectators packed the lakefront, and rooftops of downtown buildings to see competing aircraft and pilots from the United States and Europe. The performance was unpredictable. One errant pilot brushed the gilded weathervane on the 250-foot Montgomery Ward Building on Michigan Avenue.

(Opposite) At Taste of Chicago held in Grant Park every year, Chicago's restaurateurs and food vendors transform the lakefront into a giant carry-out restaurant with every imaginable food available. On the day this photo was taken, an estimated one million people visited the fest.

Cog Hill is known as home to the Western Open and as one of the toughest public courses anywhere. Located in suburban Lemont, it has become one of the most popular courses in the Chicago area. Amateurs like Michael Jordan play here, as do professionals like Tom Watson, Greg Norman and Ben Crenshaw.

(Opposite) With kickoff over two hours away, enthusiastic fans of the Chicago Bears fill the parking lot of Soldier Field for a traditional tailgate party. The aroma from countless barbeque grills, unfortunately, could not be detected in the helicopter. A promotional blimp in the shape of a giant whale seems as out of place in the air as it would be in the waters of Lake Michigan.

149

Arlington International Racecourse has new quarters after a dramatic fire in 1985 destroyed its grandstand. Management took the opportunity to upgrade, erecting a six-story stand designed by Skidmore, Owings & Merrill. Since its opening in 1927, the racetrack has been host to many celebrities, but none have been more glamorous than Secretariat who won the Arlington Invitational by nine lengths in 1973 just after he won the Triple Crown.

Hawthorne and Sportsman's parks are independent of intimate neighbors in Cicero where horse races are run in industrial surrounds.

This farmstead in the far-northwest community of South Barrington offers supplies to satisfy the most discriminating pumpkin connoisseur.

(Opposite) In 1832 Pierce Downer followed an Indian trail that led west from Chicago. After travelling twenty-five miles, he found a place that suited him and staked a claim. From this beginning Lisle has grown into a substantial suburb where the Fourth of July parade attracts a crowd of spectators.

In 1922 suburban Oak Brook was the national center for polo with a total of twenty-two playing fields. The Polo and Equestrian Club of Oak Brook, shown here, is one of the few clubs remaining in the area. It has four fields and as many as eight local teams competing regularly. Perhaps the sport's most famous player, HRH the Prince of Wales, played here in 1986.

(Opposite) Poplar Creek in suburban Hoffman Estates is a mega-auditorium. It seats 25,000 people and is used for popular road shows that can attract enormous audiences for one or two performances. Theaters like this have changed performances: at this scale, subtlety and nuance do not count for much.

Fourth of July celebrations light up the lakefront.

(Opposite) Chicago's great amusement parks — Riverview and White City — are part of the distant past. Thrill-hungry Chicagoans must take a one-hour drive northwest to Great America in Gurnee. Roller-coaster fans give high marks to the rickety looking "American Eagle" seen in the distance, although a comparison with Riverview's legendary "Bobs" might spark an argument.

Nothing escapes the scrutiny of government spy planes, even the relatively peaceful lands of the metropolitan Chicago area. This is the ultimate aerial photograph, showing the Chicago area with uncanny clarity and precision. Infrared photography makes all large areas of green foliage appear red in this remarkable view from N.A.S.A.'s U2 plane.